D1090565

STAR WARS™

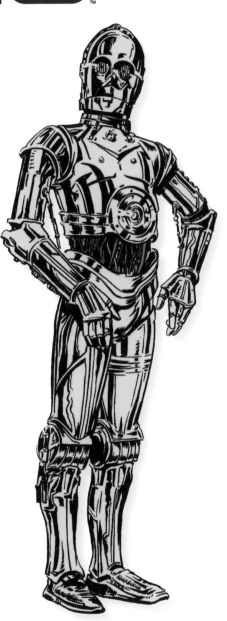

Walter Foster
Jr.

This library edition published in 2018 by Walter Foster Jr.,
an imprint of The Quarto Group
6 Orchard Road, Suite 100
Lake Forest, CA 92630

Distributed in the United States and Canada by
Lerner Publisher Services
241 First Avenue North
Minneapolis, MN 55401 U.S.A.
www.lernerbooks.com

First Library Edition

Library of Congress Cataloging-in-Publication Data

Names: Gould, Grant, illustrator.
Title: Learn to draw Star Wars / step-by-step drawings by Grant Gould.
Description: Lake Forest, CA : Published by Walter Foster Jr., an imprint of
   The Quarto Group, 2017.
Identifiers: LCCN 2017035005 | ISBN 9781942875499 (hardcover)
Subjects: LCSH: Science fiction in art. | Drawing--Technique. | Star Wars
   films.
Classification: LCC NC825.S34 L43 2017 | DDC 741.5/1--dc23
LC record available at https://lccn.loc.gov/2017035005

Printed in USA
9 8 7 6 5 4 3 2 1

Table of Contents

Tools & Materials

You need to gather only a few simple art supplies before you begin. Start with a drawing pencil and an eraser. Make sure you also have a pencil sharpener and a ruler. To add color to your drawings, use markers, colored pencils, crayons, watercolors, or acrylic paint. The choice is yours!

drawing pencil & paper

eraser

sharpener

colored pencils

felt-tip markers

paintbrushes & paints

Tracing Basics

Use tracing paper, which you can buy at your local
arts and crafts store, to trace the characters.

tracing
paper

Make sure the tracing paper is placed over
the character you want to draw. You should
be able to see through the tracing paper.

With your pencil, draw everything you can
see over the character you're tracing.

Pay close attention to all the little details.

Grid Method
Drawing Basics

When using the grid method, don't worry about the drawing as a whole. Focus on copying the lines and shapes of just one small square at a time.

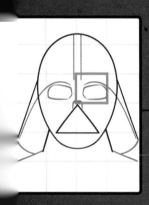 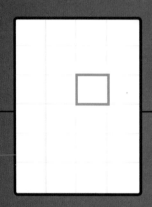 

Choose a square and copy everything into the same square on your blank practice grid. Make sure you are copying the shapes and lines into the correct spot!

After you've completed all the squares in step one, move on to the next step and keep going! Add color, and you're done!

Step-by-Step Drawing Method

When using the step-by-step drawing method, you will begin by drawing very basic shapes, such as lines and circles.

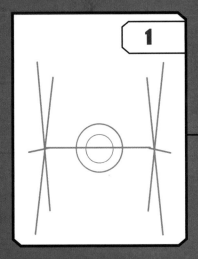

1

First draw the basic shapes, using light lines that will be easy to erase.

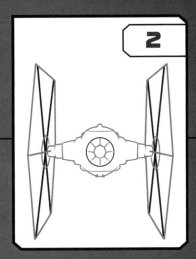

2

Pay attention to the new lines added in each step.

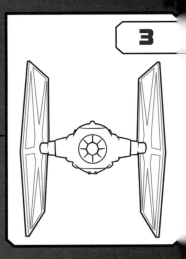

3

Erase guidelines and add more detail.

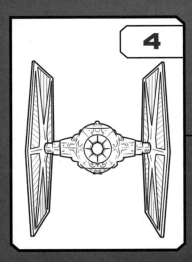

4

In each new step, add more defining lines.

5

Take your time adding detail and copying what you see.

6

Add color to your drawing with colored pencils, markers, paints, or crayons!

LUKE SKYWALKER

Luke Skywalker rose from humble beginnings as a farm boy on Tatooine to become one of the greatest Jedi the galaxy has ever known. Along with his friends Princess Leia and Han Solo, Luke battles the evil Empire, discovers the truth of who his parents are, and defeats the Sith. A generation later, the location of the famed Jedi master becomes one of the galaxy's greatest mysteries.

Abilities & Equipment

- **Strong with the Force**
- **Trained under Obi-Wan Kenobi and Master Yoda**
- **Skilled with a lightsaber**
- **Can move heavy objects with his mind by using the Force**
- **Expert pilot**

TRACE LUKE SKYWALKER ON TRANSPARENT PAPER.

LUKE SKYWALKER

STEP ONE

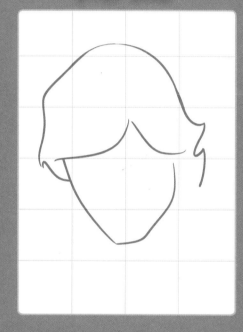

STEP TWO

STEP THREE

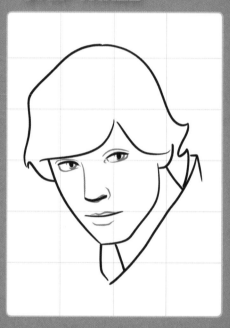

STEP FOUR

STEP FIVE

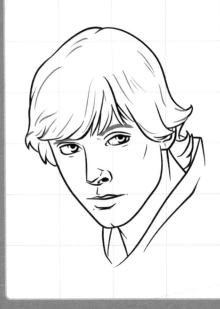

STEP SIX

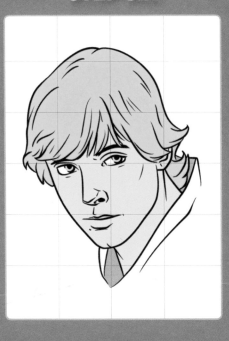

LUKE SKYWALKER

1

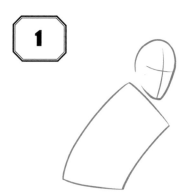

2

Use basic shapes to start your drawing, copy the new lines
in each step, darken the lines you want to keep, and erase the rest.
Add color with colored pencils, markers, paints, or crayons.

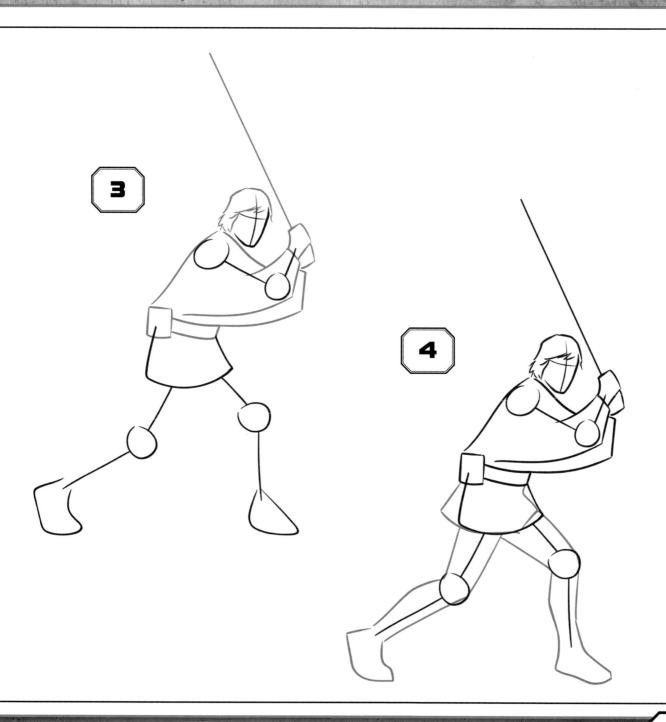

LUKE SKYWALKER

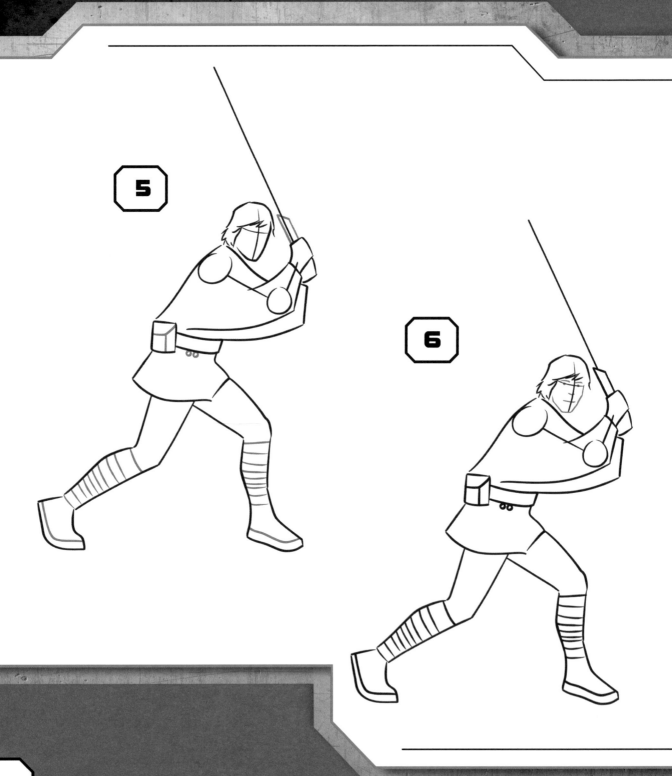

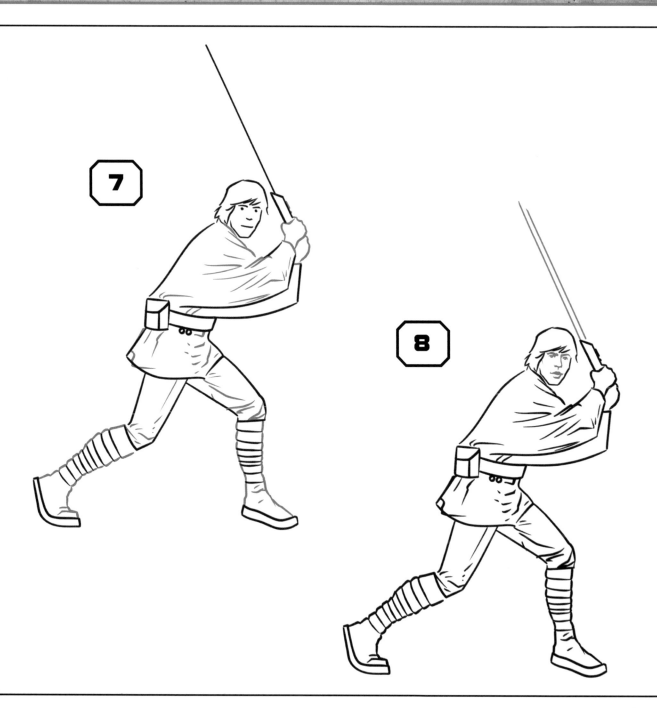

LUKE SKYWALKER

NOW ADD COLOR.

11

R2-D2

A resourceful astromech droid, R2-D2 serves Padmé Amidala, Anakin Skywalker, and Luke Skywalker in turn, showing great bravery in rescuing his masters and their friends from many dangers. A skilled starship mechanic and fighter pilot's assistant, Artoo forms an unlikely but enduring friendship with the fussy protocol droid C-3PO.

Abilities & Equipment

- Trustworthy secret-keeper
- Can hook into any computer system
- Equipped with holoprojector and recorder for Rebel messages
- Carries a rocket booster

TRACE R2-D2 ON TRANSPARENT PAPER.

R2-D2

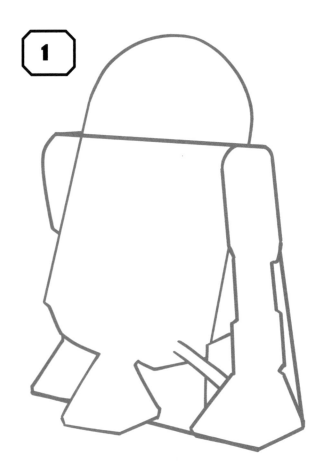

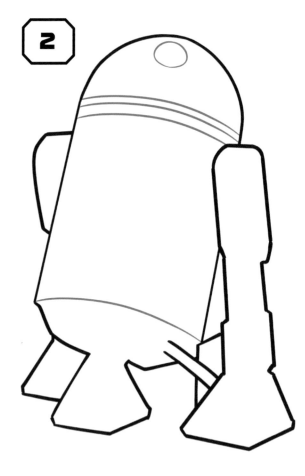

Use basic shapes to start your drawing, copy the new lines in each step, darken the lines you want to keep, and erase the rest. Add color with colored pencils, markers, paints, or crayons.

3

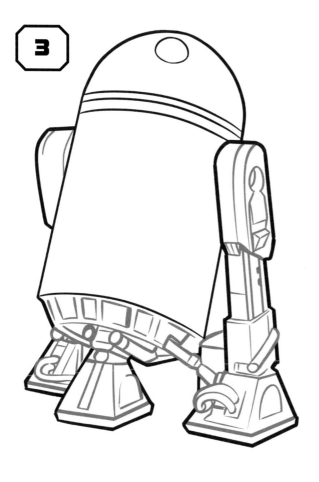

4

R2-D2

5

6

NOW ADD COLOR.

7

C-3PO

Built by Anakin Skywalker, C-3PO is a droid programmed for etiquette and protocol. A constant companion to R2-D2, Threepio is involved in some of the galaxy's most defining moments and thrilling battles.

Abilities & Equipment

- Diplomatic
- Specializes in human-cyborg relations
- Fluent in over 6 million forms of communication
- Able to calculate complicated odds instantaneously
- Programmed in protocol

TRACE C-3PO ON
TRANSPARENT PAPER.

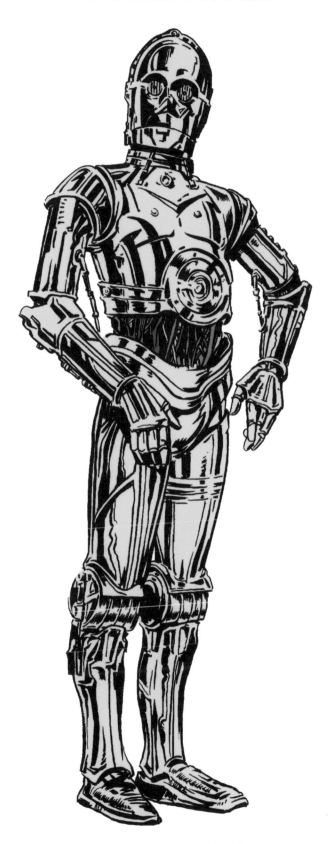

C-3PO

STEP ONE   **STEP TWO**   **STEP THREE**

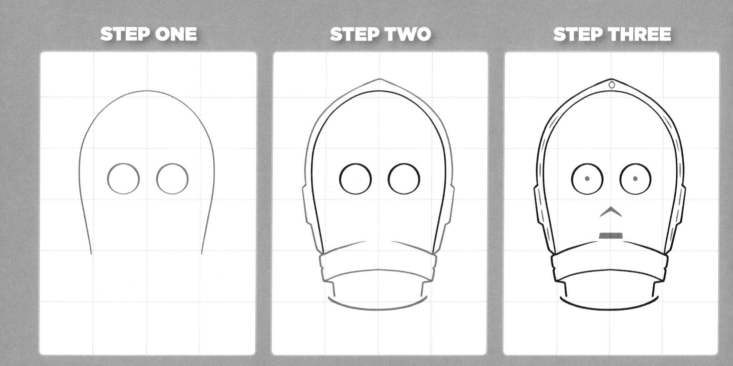

STEP FOUR

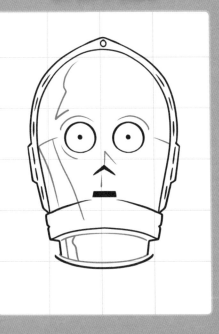

STEP FIVE

STEP SIX

HAN SOLO

Smuggler. Scoundrel. Hero. Han Solo, captain of the *Millennium Falcon*, is one of the great leaders of the Rebel Alliance. He and his co-pilot Chewbacca come to believe in the cause of galactic freedom, joining Luke Skywalker and Princess Leia Organa in the fight against the Empire.

Abilities & Equipment

- Captain of the *Millennium Falcon*, a ship so fast it made the Kessel Run in less than 12 parsecs
- Talented pilot
- Lightning-fast reflexes and a good shot with a blaster
- Deeply loyal to friends and the Rebel Alliance

Use basic shapes to start your drawing, copy the new lines
in each step, darken the lines you want to keep, and erase the rest.
Add color with colored pencils, markers, paints, or crayons.

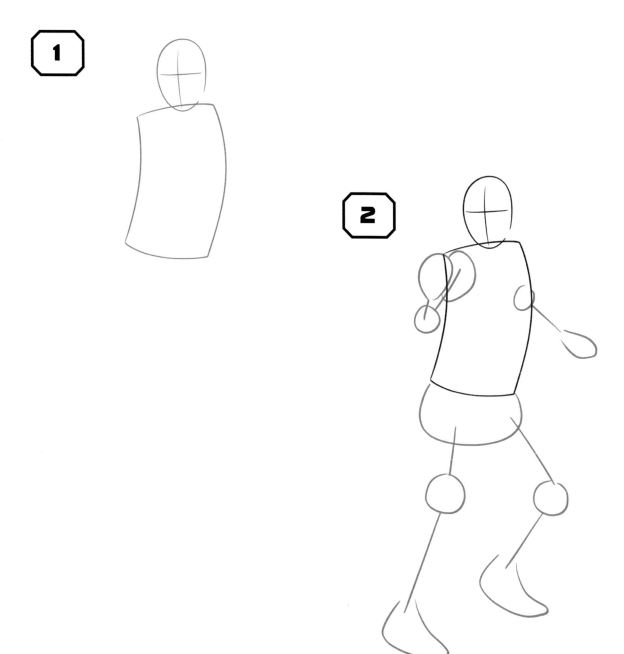

1

2

HAN SOLO

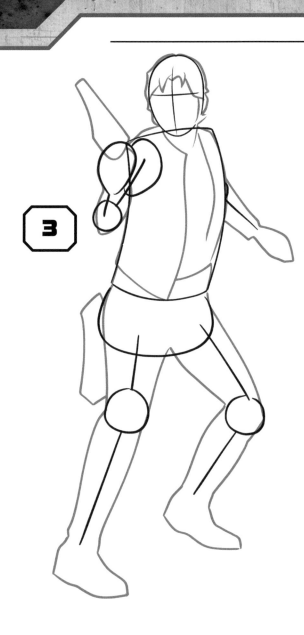

3

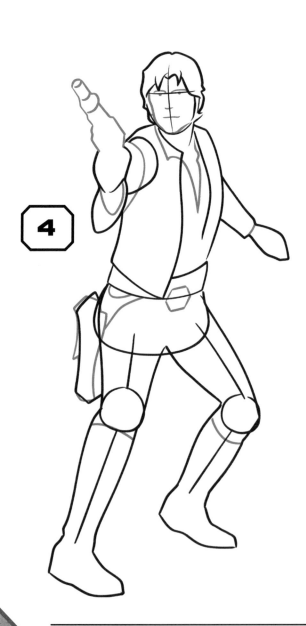

4

5

6

HAN SOLO

NOW ADD COLOR.

9

CHEWBACCA

A legendary Wookiee warrior and Han Solo's co-pilot aboard the *Millennium Falcon*, Chewbacca is part of a core group of Rebels who restore freedom to the galaxy. Known for his short temper and accuracy with a bowcaster, Chewie also has a big heart—and is unwavering in his loyalty to his friends.

Abilities & Equipment

- **Co-pilot of the *Millennium Falcon***
- **Skilled with a bowcaster**
- **Master mechanic**
- **Devoted and caring friend**

Use basic shapes to start your drawing, copy the new lines in each step, darken the lines you want to keep, and erase the rest. Add color with colored pencils, markers, paints, or crayons.

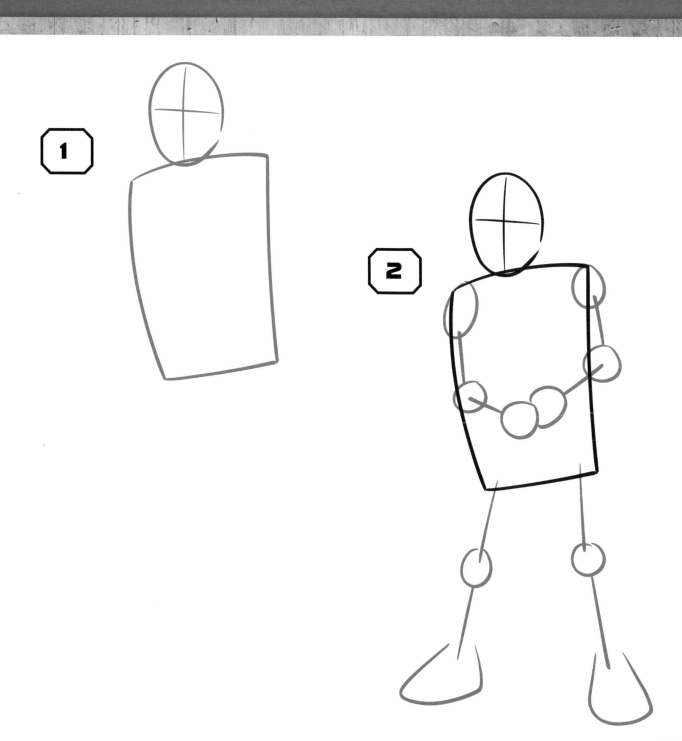

1

2

CHEWBACCA

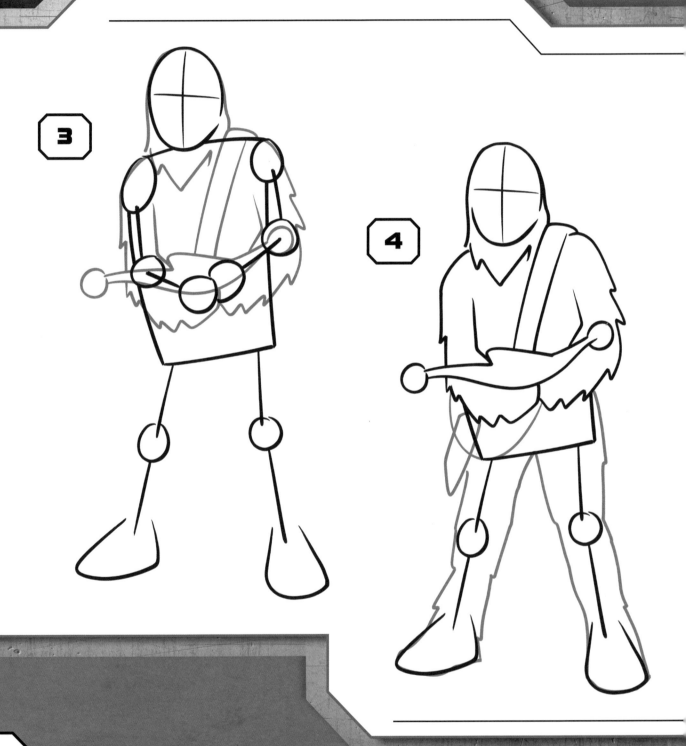

3

4

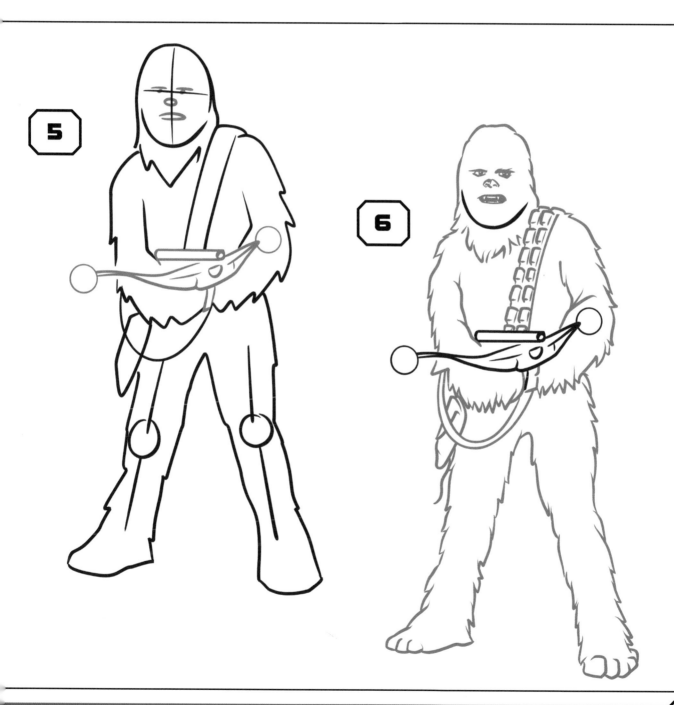

CHEWBACCA

7

8

NOW ADD COLOR.

9

PRINCESS LEIA

Leia Organa is one of the Rebel Alliance's greatest leaders, fearless on the battlefield and dedicated to fighting the Empire. Her impressive résumé begins with the title of Princess of Alderaan, but later she becomes a member of the Imperial Senate, a leader in the Rebel Alliance, and the founding general of the Resistance.

Abilities & Equipment

- Strong, dedicated leader with sharp wit
- Force-sensitive
- Great accuracy with blaster pistols
- Renowned for her diplomatic skills, a capable mediator

Use basic shapes to start your drawing, copy the new lines in each step, darken the lines you want to keep, and erase the rest. Add color with colored pencils, markers, paints, or crayons.

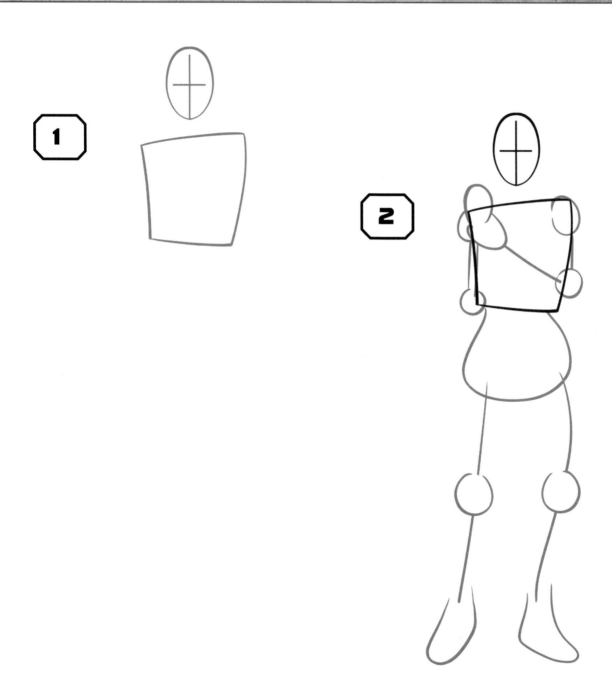

PRINCESS LEIA

3

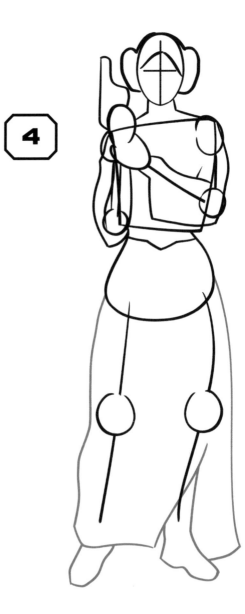

4

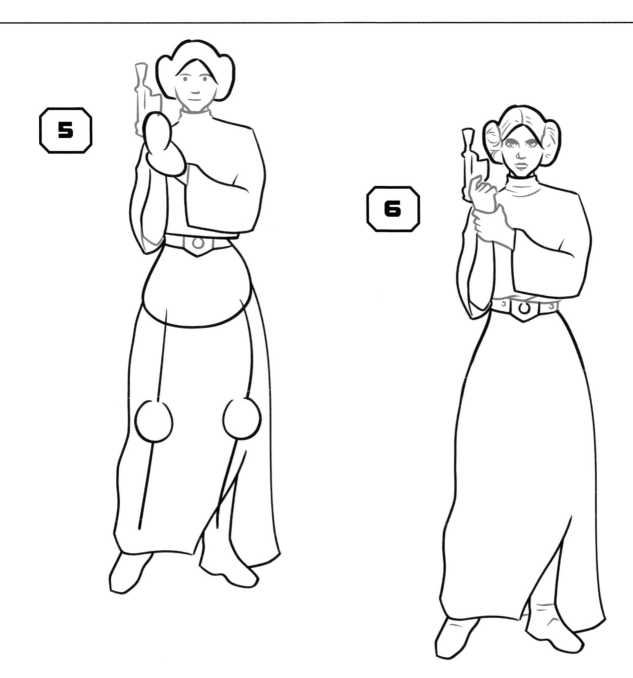

PRINCESS LEIA

7

8

NOW ADD COLOR.

9

DARTH VADER

Once a heroic Jedi Knight, Darth Vader is seduced by the dark side of the Force, becomes a Sith Lord, and leads the Empire's fight against the Jedi Order. He remains in service of the Emperor—the evil Darth Sidious—for decades, enforcing his Master's will and seeking to crush the fledgling Rebel Alliance. But there is still good in him...

Abilities & Equipment

- Gifted pilot and podracer
- One of the most powerful Jedi in the galaxy, until joining the dark side
- Skilled with his red-bladed lightsaber
- Can inflict harm through the Force
- Wears intimidating armor to protect his severely injured body

TRACE DARTH VADER ON TRANSPARENT PAPER.

DARTH VADER

1

2

Use basic shapes to start your drawing, copy the new lines in each step, darken the lines you want to keep, and erase the rest. Add color with colored pencils, markers, paints, or crayons.

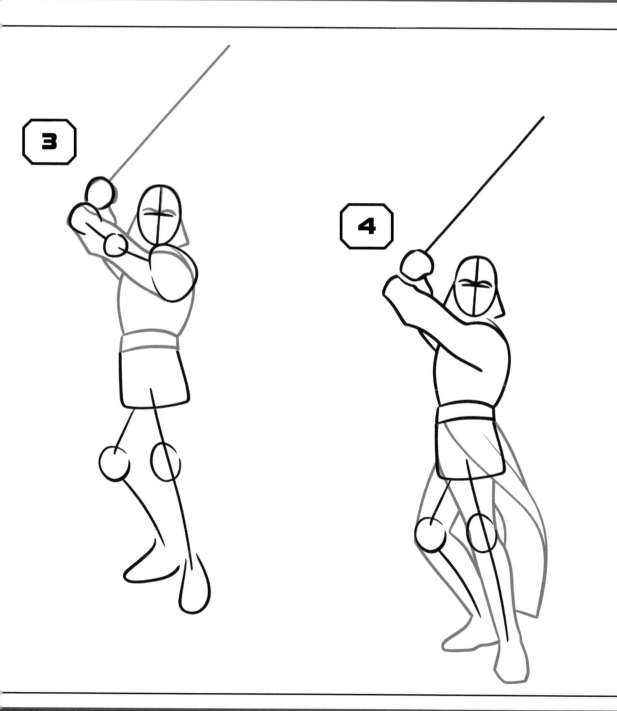

DARTH VADER

5

6

7

DARTH VADER

8

NOW ADD COLOR.

9

STORMTROOPER

Stormtroopers are shock troops fanatically loyal to the Empire and nearly impossible to sway from the Imperial cause. They wear imposing white armor, wield blaster rifles and pistols, and attack in hordes to overwhelm their enemies.

Abilities & Equipment

- **Trained for total obedience**
- **Will fight to the death for the Emperor, even when the odds are against them**
- **Wear white armor with survival equipment and temperature controls**
- **Fight with blaster pistols, blaster rifles, AT-AT Walkers, etc.**

TRACE THE STORMTROOPER
ON TRANSPARENT PAPER.

STORMTROOPER

STEP ONE

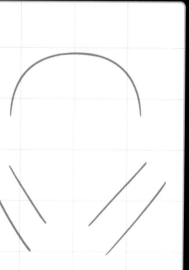

STEP TWO

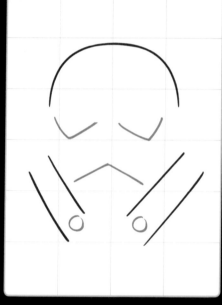

STEP THREE

STEP FOUR

STEP FIVE

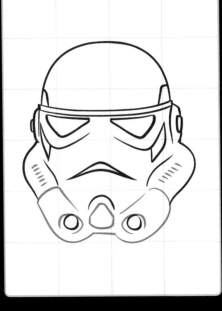

STEP SIX

YODA

Yoda is a legendary Jedi Master and stronger than most in his connection with the Force. Despite being only 2.2 feet tall and almost 900 years old, Yoda is wise and powerful. Although he is an exceptionally skilled and acrobatic fighter, Yoda is most of all an advisor and teacher, serving on the Jedi High Council and training Jedi for more than 800 years.

Abilities & Equipment

- **Fights with a smaller green lightsaber**
- **Employs acrobatics in combat, despite his old age**
- **Can move heavy objects and communicate with his mind by using the Force.**
- **Can see visions of the future**

Use basic shapes to start your drawing, copy the new lines
in each step, darken the lines you want to keep, and erase the rest.
Add color with colored pencils, markers, paints, or crayons.

1

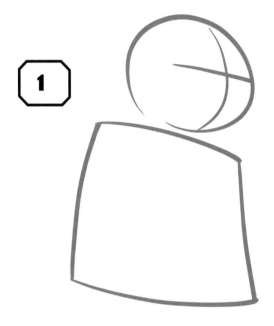

2

YODA

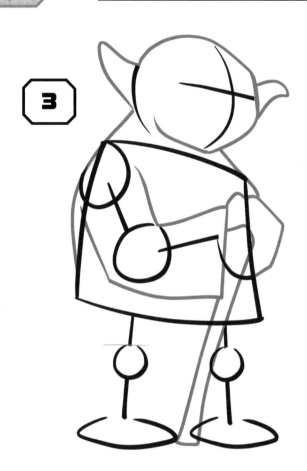

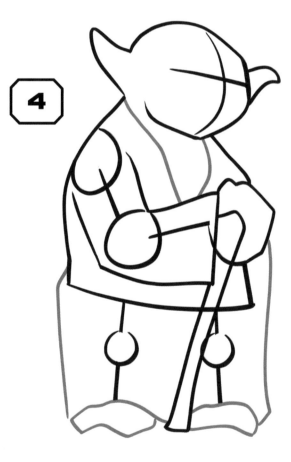

5

6

YODA

7

8

NOW ADD COLOR.

9

THE END